"We must not, in trying to think about how we can make a big difference, ignore the small daily differences we can make which, over time, add up to big differences that we often cannot foresee."
- Marian Wright Edelman

The 48 Laws of Black Empowerment

The 48 Laws of Black Empowerment

The concept of black unity has been a fleeting dream for the last 400 years. If we look at history, it seems that the longer we spend in America, the more divided we become. When black families were split up, other slaves became their family out of the necessity of survival. But it seems that the more freedoms we get, the more we want to hold each other back, tear each other down, and kill each other off. That's not by accident, but by design. The same tactics used by the slave masters and politicians to tear us apart, can also be used to "reverse engineer" our problems. We don't have to riot, rally, or revolt to make any of these changes happen. There's no group to infiltrate with COINTELPRO, no movement to demonize, and no leadership to kill off or imprison. Not only is black unity achievable, but it is achievable in as little time as it takes for you to digest the ideas presented in this book, apply them to your life, and then pass them on. To get where we want to go, we only need to focus on making small adjustments to the following areas of our life:

1. Personal
2. Family
3. Business & Finance
4. Community
5. Activism

In the 1960s the original Black Panthers put together a common sense Ten Point Program for the black community, which has gone ignored in discussions on how we progress as a people. They also put together Eight Points of Attention, seven of which are on life support in our culture.

1. Speak politely.
2. Pay fairly for what you buy.
3. Return everything you borrow.
4. Pay for anything you damage.
5. Do not hit or swear at people.

6. Don't damage property or crops of the poor, oppressed masses.
7. Do not take liberties with women.

In this book you'll find influences from the Black Panthers, The 50th Law, Marcus Garvey, and many others. The collective black consciousness has given us a road map to change, but it is up to follow it.

> **"I have discovered in life that there are ways of getting almost anywhere you want to go, if you really want to go." – Langston Hughes**

PERSONAL

We can't change the world around us until we make changes to ourselves. It goes back to the saying, "lead by example." People's friends tend to reflect who they are, which is why the following sayings were created:

- Show me who your friends are and I'll show you who you are.
- Birds of a feather flock together.
- One rotten apple spoils the whole bunch.

The way we think, the way we behave, the energy we put out, and the way we respond are all choices made by us on a daily basis. By taking a more conscious approach to several areas of our lives, those changes will carry over into other areas outside of personal, and manifest into positive results in our family and community.

> **"If you don't like something, change it. If you can't change it, change your attitude."**
> **– Maya Angelou**

#1. All Praises To The Most High

God over everything. We are naturally spiritual people. Christianity, Black Hebrew Israelites, Islam, Jehovah's Witnesses, Kemet, and ancestral religions all share a common belief that there is something more than the natural world we see. Very rarely do we find a true atheist among us, which is why we must all put our faith in The Most High God.

The root cause of our spiritual division is our inability to agree on the true name of God. Is it Yah, Jehovah, or Allah? To that question, the Bible offers a valuable piece of wisdom. When Moses asked God what his name was, he was given the name "Jehovah" in the KJV. But he also revealed to Moses that he was not known to Abraham, Isaac, and Jacob by that name, but by the name "God Almighty".

If we were able to put Moses and Abraham in a room together and ask them the name of The Most High God, they'd give different answers (all theological arguments for why it couldn't happen aside). They could debate as long as they wanted, and they'd all be right about their own argument, but they'd all be wrong about the other person's position even though they served the same God. By using the title "The Most High" we remove one of our barriers to unity.

Cultural Importance

When our ancestors were brought to America, they had their faith stripped, and were then taught a Eurocentric interpretation of the Bible. They didn't want us praying to The Most High, so they replaced him with their own likeness so we'd look to them as saviors.

> **"So I say to you, seek God, and discover Him and make Him a power in your life. Without Him all of our efforts turn to ashes and our sunrises**

into darkest nights. Without Him, life is a meaningless drama with the decisive scenes missing. But with him we are able to rise from the fatigue of despair to the buoyancy of hope. With Him we are able to rise from the midnight of desperation to the daybreak of Joy. St. Augustine was right, we were made for God and we will be restless until we find rest in Him." – Dr. Martin Luther King Jr.

#2. Know Your Identity

Almost all of our history has been hidden, lied about, or white washed into non existence, but there are enough remaining fragments to piece together what actually happened. There are maps, journal entries, newspaper clippings, and historical descriptions that the internet has become a repository of information. If we look at the evidence subjectively, there are only a few possible conclusions that can be drawn from it. A great place to start researching is with the 1747 map of Africa created by Emanuel Bowen as part of his last collection. After that, there is a 1766 French map created for the Duke of Orleans that contains notes about our identity.

We've been so caught up with chasing our true identity that we often overlook what's right in front of our face. Knowing who we are and where we come from will put a lot of our current economic and political problems into perspective.

Cultural Importance

Our ancestors had their names stripped, they were forbidden from speaking their original language, and families were split up. In addition to this, most documents before and during the slave trade were destroyed to cover up what the Europeans were doing. They didn't want us to remember our identity.

> **"As long as we are not ourselves, we will try to be what other people are."**
> **- Malidoma Patrice Somé**

#3. Be Yourself

A certain kind of pride comes with learning the truth about who we are, but that's a journey that we each have to make for ourselves. The entire world, but especially America, is built on the European idea of beauty and acceptance. We will never fit those standards no matter how hard we try because they aren't meant for us to meet.

Far too many of try to be like them and mimic them. Some of our women straighten their hair like their women, some of our men try to carry themselves like their men, and almost all of us have used code switching to sound more like they sound. The irony of it is that their women are getting implants, injections, tans, and surgery to look like our women. Their men are embracing hip hop to be more like our men. If we're trying to be more like them, and their goal is to be like us, then we should just be ourselves.

Cultural Importance

It is becoming more difficult for this generation to simply exist. Police are called on us just for being black, our hairstyles are banned, and we are almost always depicted in a negative light by the media. Now more than ever we need to reinforce the idea that it is OK to be who we are.

> **"It is the duty of the younger Negro artist to change through the force of his art that old**

> **whispering 'I want to be white,' hidden in the aspirations of his people, to 'Why should I be white? I am a Negro—and beautiful!'**
> **- Langston Hughes**

#4. Embrace Education

It is not the European's responsibility to educated us or our children. In order for us to educate others, we must first educate ourselves. Not only do we need to know their version of history for academic purposes, but we also need to know ACTUAL history for ourselves. European history is always revisionist to favor them. We know that people were in America and coming to America long before it was "discovered" by Columbus. We know that slavery was pure evil, our ancestors worked for free, and yet they refuse to acknowledge how much it devastated us as a nation.

Once we educate ourselves, we need to educate our family, friends, and others in the community. Being intelligent shouldn't be a bulliable offense, nor should it be looked at as a weakness. Our ancestors built the pyramids and they built this nation. We aren't a dumb people and the perception of us needs to reflect that. When others make the assumption that we're less intelligent than we are, being smart will give us an intellectual advantage, whether on the block or in the board room.

Cultural Importance

Our ancestors were forbidden to learn how to read or write, under penalty of fines, beatings, and death. Now that we are able to freely obtain an education, we should do so. This does not always mean obtaining a formal education at an expensive university. It is perfectly OK to educate ourselves in areas where the school system is lacking or missing altogether.

> **"I think education is power. I think that being able to communicate with people is power. One of my main goals on the planet is to encourage people to empower themselves."**
> **– Oprah Winfrey**

#5. Celebrate Black History Every Month

This goes hand in hand with general education. Learning just a couple of things related to our history every month can be an eye opening experience. Our culture is rich with inventers, artists, innovators, heroes, and even villains. Black history is too vast to cover in a period of 30 days per year, and they're currently trying to dilute it even more into Diversity Month. We don't need the approval of people that don't look like us in order to celebrate our own history. We also shouldn't expect them to handle it with the amount of care or accuracy that we would for ourselves.

Ourselves and our children need to understand that we can do more than handle a ball, rap, dance, sell drugs, pimp, hustle, and entertain people that don't look like us. Our people are some of the smartest people on the planet. The following are just a few black inventions that get overlooked every Black History month:

- Transport Refrigeration was invented by Frederick M. Jones.
- Open Heart Surgery was invented by Daniel Hale Williams.
- Traffic Lights were invented by Garrett Morgan.
- Light Bulb Filament was invented by Lewis Latimer.
- Synthesis of Medicinal Drugs from Plants (the entire modern pharmaceutical industry) was invented by Percy Lavon Julian.

It's not the responsibility of people that don't look like us to teach our history to us or our children. It is the responsibility of black parents to teach black children about black history.

Cultural Importance

Most of our history was covered up to hide who we are. The contributions of black Americans are always downplayed and under celebrated to make our accomplishments seem insignificant in to the story of American history.

> **"The writer cannot expect to be excused from the task of reeducation and regeneration that must be done. In fact, he should march right in front." - Chinua Achebe**

#6. Never Underestimate Street Smarts

If asked, most people will acknowledge that there is a difference between book smarts and street smarts. Book smarts can get us far in specific situations, but streets smarts can get us where we need to go throughout our lives. Book smarts help us determine the facts, but streets smarts alert us to the shady lawyer, manager, or whoever that's trying to get over on us in a deal.

Those of us that possess book smarts and streets smarts will often get further than those that only possess one or the other. Some examples of people that I perceive to be both book smart and street smart would be Master P, T.I., Jay Z, 50 Cent, Birdman, and Puffy. Coming from a background in hip hop, these were the black business men that I looked up to for inspiration. Together these men have made BILLIONS for their investors, themselves, their families, their organizations, and the communities they give back to. No matter what we think of them in their personal lives, we should all aspire to achieve epic levels of success as they have.

Cultural Importance

Most of our survival in America and other parts of the world has been based on street smarts. Our ancestors were forced to survive in a land without their own resources, language, or the ability to read and write. Many of us alive today do not have degrees or a formal education. Most of what we know we've learned from living life. Never take this for granted because many people that don't have street smarts are passed up by those that do.

> **"Not a Harvard-type education, ... Just a not-sticking-up-a-liquor-store-type education."**
> **– Chris Rock**

#7. Know Your Strengths and Weaknesses

A logical person understand that we all have our strengths and weaknesses. A person that knows who they are, possesses book smarts, and street smarts can identify what their strengths and weaknesses are. One of the hardest things to do is honestly assess ourselves. We'd all love to believe that we are better people than we are in certain areas, but we aren't perfect, and that's perfectly fine.

Once we assess ourselves, we can start to make our weak points stronger, and our strong points even better. If you know someone that is strong in an area in where you're weak, learn from them or learn to work with them so that you can help each other compensate. In fact, if you're comfortable enough, assess each other to see what others perceive your weaknesses to be. This will only lead to more personal growth in the future. If you're in business, it's important to know when to hire someone stronger than you in certain areas. Taxes is one of these areas. Know your limitations. Successful people don't get to where they are by trying to do everything alone. No man is an island, and successful people build teams to that make each other stronger.

> **"If you don't understand yourself you don't understand anybody else." - Nikki Giovanni**

#8. Know When To Be A Follower

Everyone wants to be the HNIC and that's understandable in most circumstances, but there's no shame in knowing when to follow the lead of someone else. The Alpha mentality is what holds a lot of our progress back. We make it about competing to see who's an Alpha and who's Beta, but with no clear plan where the Alpha intends to lead. If you don't have a plan to lead, then follow, and help the leader get to where they're leading, to the best of your ability.

Being a follower isn't always a bad thing. If your child was hurt and a doctor told you exactly what to do, would you play Alpha and refuse to take orders or would you do everything in your power to follow their directions exactly as given so that you could help your child? We would all do the latter. We should take this same attitude when it comes to our own people. This ties back into knowing our strengths and weaknesses.

Cultural Importance

People like MLK and Malcolm X wouldn't be who they are if it weren't for their supporters. Harriet Tubman couldn't have led people to freedom if they weren't willing to follow.

> **"And he spake a parable unto them, Can the blind lead the blind? shall they not both fall into the ditch?" – Luke 6:39**

#9. Question Your Pastor

Knowing who to follow is just as important as allowing yourself to follow. In the black church it is considered borderline blasphemy to question a black pastor. It doesn't matter which religion you follow, you need to question the leader when the leader behaves or teaches in a manner that doesn't lead to the betterment of our people. While you should double check all doctrine, this is more so about how the money is handled.

Ask if you can sit in on a board meeting or a financial meeting if your place of worship offers it. If not, ask if you can see the books. It's your money and you have the right to know where it's going. If they refuse, then take your money elsewhere. If it seems like they're misusing or misappropriating funds, take your money elsewhere. For far too long, hustlers in suits have been using the black community as a personal piggy bank by posing as preachers, prophets, and apostles. They then take that money and spend it on luxuries made by people that don't look like us. This has to stop and we don't have to say a word. All we have to do is remove our money from the equation and their scam will fall apart. If you do have a chance to sit in and everything looks on the up and up, then continue to support your place of worship, especially if it's within our community. We can weed out the good and bad by make the personal decision to stop financially enabling wolves in sheep's clothing.

Cultural Importance

Black church leadership has historically been viewed by the United States government and other organizations as a means of controlling the black community. Black pastors were paid off and indoctrinated to disseminate ideas that were of benefit to Europeans, but of detriment to black Americans.

> **"But there were false prophets also among the people, even as there shall be false teachers among you, who privily shall bring in damnable heresies, even denying the Lord that bought them, and bring upon themselves swift destruction." – 2 Peter 2:1**

#10. Embrace Technology

It seems like our people are always the last to embrace new technologies. Not only do we need to educate ourselves about what technology is available to us, but we also need to start learning how to implement that technology into our businesses and personal lives beyond being a consumer. More of us need to learn how to build our own websites, get our products listed on Amazon, get our music on Spotify, publish our own books, integrate affiliate programs into our online businesses, and more. The further we fall behind when it comes to embracing technology, the further the wealth gap will get.

Every major social network and ecommerce site is owned by people that don't look like us. While it's unrealistic to think that Facebook or Amazon are going away any time soon, it shouldn't stop us from building our own online communities that serve our needs. We don't need to create another Facebook, but there's nothing stopping us from creating our own local websites that serve as media outlets to share our news from our perspectives.

How others use technology isn't necessarily meant to cater to us. We need to start developing platforms, apps, and other ways of serving our own businesses and communities better.

Cultural Importance

We don't want our people to fall behind. Historically, we're responsible for most of the technologies that have allowed America and other parts of the world to thrive. We need to continue on in this legacy by being innovators of technology and not just adopters.

> **"I am a woman who came from the cotton fields of the South. From there, I was promoted to the washtub. From there, I was promoted to the cook kitchen. And from there, I promoted myself into the business of manufacturing hair goods and preparations. I have built my own factory on my own ground."**
> **- Madam C.J. Walker**

#11. Know Your Worth

One of my favorite stories is how Master P turned down a million dollar offer because he knew that if he was being offered a million, he was worth a lot more. Our entertainers are often low balled in their contracts because those companies understand our worth. Because of our experiences we often undervalue ourselves if it seems like the opportunity being presented can change our situation for the better.

If you currently work a 9 – 5, set a realistic minimum hourly amount that you want and get it. If you own a business, figure out how much you want to make and make it happen. If you're an entertainer and you're being offered 15%, and you know you can match that on your own with

1/6 of the fans, go independent and cut out the middle man completely. Don't sign anything or accept any job that undervalues you. That's how they've been getting rich off of us since the beginning. It is the same mentality that prevents them from paying reparations to us, while they pay them to everyone else they've done wrong. They know our worth but don't want to pay us what we're worth.

Cultural Importance

People don't enslave people for 400 years if they aren't worth anything. Europeans have made money off of everything we've created. From the cotton gin to rap music, they've known how much money we could potentially generate for them from the start. We are not worthless as they've led many of us to believe.

> **"The outside world told black kids when I was growing up that we weren't worth anything. But our parents said it wasn't so, and our churches and our school teachers said it wasn't so. They believed in us, and we, therefore, believed in ourselves." – Marian Wright Edelman**

#12. Stop Waiting For Black Leaders

The problem with black leadership is that there isn't any at the moment. There are pockets of people that will rally if urged by celebrities, but those celebrities aren't really taking on the responsibility of black leadership, nor should they. If we look at what happened with the election of Barack Obama to the presidency, black celebrities were waiting to follow his lead (Law #8). When he ran his campaign, even people that are traditionally in leadership roles played their part to support what he was trying to accomplish. We even saw Oprah play a supporting role for the greater cause, which was getting Barack Obama elected as the first black president.

Now that President Obama is out of office, we've gone dormant again, waiting for the next big thing to jump behind and support. We need to stop waiting for black leaders to stand up and move us to action. The problem with President Obama is that he was the only person that looked like him running for office. Our community should've been so motivated that he would've had to compete with five other people that looked just like him. We need to become the leaders that we're waiting for.

Cultural Importance

Traditionally black leaders have come in the form of men of faith. Many leaders in the church today don't want to rock the boat or lose members, so our expectation for a black leader with an unapologetically black cause should be low. Movements will come and go, but the black leaders of the past may just be a thing of the past.

> **"Change will not come if we wait for some other person or some other time. We are the ones we've been waiting for. We are the change that we seek." — Barack Obama**

#13. Don't Let People Kill Your Dreams

Our ability to dream is what pushes us to be more than what we are. Unfortunately, there are haters in the world that try to kill our dreams just because we expressed them. When I use the term hater, I'm not using it in the general popular over use of the word to describe anyone that doesn't like you, but in a more specific way. When a person tells you that you can't do something or tries to discourage you, it means that they either don't have faith in your ability or they don't want you to succeed. Either way, that person is not in your corner and you need to get rid of them, regardless of who they are.

Allowing these people to remain around us or have access to us will ultimately bring us down and prevent us from achieving our goals. They will bad mouth you to others, leak information about you for money, and anything else they can do to sabotage you in the long run. Let these people watch you succeed at a distance.

Cultural Importance

This was literal just a few decades ago. Dreams of getting an education alongside white kids or being able to date anyone we wanted got many of our people killed. Now that those times are over, we need to make sure to honor their sacrifice by always striving to achieve ours.

> **"Every great dream begins with a dreamer. Always remember, you have within you the strength, the patience, and the passion to reach for the stars to change the world."**
> **– Harriet Tubman**

#14. Change Your Mentality

At some point the phrases "that's not how I was raised" and "that's just how I was raised", need to be done away with. These are just commonly accepted excuses for not taking accountability for our choices. I'm willing to bet that the majority of us were not raised to drink, do drugs, and make babies before marriage, but we still managed to overcome our upbringing and get it done anyway.

Our upbringing and environment only influence our outcome so much. It's more about mentality than circumstance. One person may be told, "you'll never make it as a comedian", and they believe it. Another kid will get told the same thing, and they'll think to themselves, "I'm going to prove you wrong and rub it in your face." There are probably deeper psychological reasons as to why they develop a different mentality, but how they choose to think is more important than how they were raised.

If we change the way we think, we'll start to recognize when we're making excuses for not doing certain things. If there's a legitimate reason why we can't do something, we should refer back to Law #7 and compensate for it. If there's something we don't know, we need to educate ourselves. "I don't know how to do that" is no longer an acceptable answer since the advent of Google and YouTube. If we don't know it's because we don't want to know. If we don't fix our weaknesses it's because we don't want to. If we don't know our identity, it's because we don't want to know it. The time for excuses is over. From here on out, if we choose not to do something it simply because we don't want to do it, and for no other reason (physical handicaps excluded).

Cultural Importance

During slavery, children were raised to always address white people a certain way, always behave a certain way around white people, and never ask questions. At some point our people stopped thinking that way. Just because we're raised a certain way doesn't mean we have to be bound to that way of life, especially if it's not beneficial to us, our family, or community.

> **"What you're supposed to do when you don't like a thing is change it. If you can't change it, change the way you think about it."**
> **– Maya Angelou**

FAMILY

Our family is the very first community that we get to know. How we grow up will often shape our perceptions about relationships and parenting. For those with non traditional families made up of people unrelated by blood, some of those bonds become much tighter than the bonds those of us with blood relatives often form. No matter what type of family dynamic we have, we must always strive to keep the black family intact.

For years the U.S. government has attacked the black family through various policies on both the Democrat and the Republican sides. Family unity is the cornerstone of black empowerment. A supportive family dynamic has the power to push us further than we've ever dreamed possible.

> **"Never exalt people because they're your family, never exalt people because they're your color... Exalt them because they're worthy."**
> **- Louis Farrakhan**

#15. Support The Black Family Dynamic

Our culture is obsessed with being independent to the point that the term is overused and misused. I refer to myself as an independent author, but in reality, I depend on a company to print my books, package my books, and ship my books. This makes me interdependent. Interdependent is what we all are. Independent musicians depend on their team of people to help them succeed. Independent filmmakers depend on actors to bring their project to life on the screen.

It is the myth of independence that has led to the glamorization of single parents. We glorify being a "baby mama" or "single mother" over being a wife. We glorify being a "baby daddy" or "single father" over being a husband. We throw divorce parties as if that's something to be proud of. To incentivize this, the Welfare system often pays out more money to black women without a man living in the house. If they can get more money without the father in the house, what do they need the father for? They could just as easily offer the incentive to keep the family together, but that wasn't the agenda. This was purposely done to tear apart the black family. This isn't said to blame the black woman, but it was a very real and strategic move by the United States government to destroy the black family dynamic.

Another problem we have in our community is the failure to build a family decently and in order. We date, have kids, break up, and then find someone other than the child's parent to marry. That's not an accident, nor is it a mistake. Every decision was made to do those things in that order, whether or not we intend them to turn out that way. This goes back to Law #14. We don't exchange numbers by accident, go on dates by accident, have unprotected sex by accident, or cheat by accident. All of those things are choices that we need to own and fix. Children don't decide whether or not they grow up in a household with a married mother and father, we do. If we want to create a family dynamic, then we need to marry BEFORE we have children. This means that we choose to either abstain from sex or ONLY have protected sex until we can create the environment in which we want our children born into. Anything other than that is just an excuse.

Cultural Importance

During slavery, families were split up and sold off to other plantations never to see each other again. In a lot of ways the black family is just as divided as it was then. We need to change the level of importance we place on family to extend beyond blood relatives. We need to think of family in terms of the men and women we choose to have children with. If we view those people as family, and not just "baby mamas" and "baby daddies", then we may begin to see more black households in which the mother and father are present.

> **"The breakdown of the black community, in order to maintain slavery, began with the breakdown of the black family. Men and women were not legally allowed to get married because you couldn't have that kind of love. It might get in the way of the economics of slavery. Your children could be taken from you and literally sold down the river." – Kerry Washington**

#16. Choose Your Family Wisely

As we get older, we become more selective about who we deal with in our personal lives. Sometimes we make friends that become closer than blood relatives, and sometimes blood relatives aren't the kind of people we choose to be around. However your family dynamic is made up, choose people that route for you to succeed. If someone is trying to hold you back, discourage you, or doesn't believe in you, remove that person from your inner circle. We need to shake the belief that blood relation gives our family the right to say and do whatever they want to negatively affect us, and we just have to deal with it. We don't and we shouldn't.

Cultural Importance

When families were split up, our ancestors were forced to find family among strangers. Those new families turned into every black person we see today. We are all family. To paraphrase the Bible, "better is a friend that is close than a brother that is far away."

> "Do not bring people in your life who weigh you down. And trust your instincts ... good relationships feel good. They feel right. They don't hurt. They're not painful. That's not just with somebody you want to marry, but it's with the friends that you choose. It's with the people you surround yourselves with."
> – Michelle Obama

#17. Show Up For Our People

The world is against us, so whenever our people accomplish something we need to show up and support. We may not make every event, but we should strive to support them as much as possible, especially if we expect them to support us when we accomplish something great. It doesn't matter if your cousin just dropped a country music album and you hate everything about country. Show up anyway and support their dream.

Once we show up, we need to take it a step further if the situation allows. If they've just released an album, book, or movie, help them by sharing it on social media, help work a table to sell stuff, or whatever it takes. Be their biggest support so that when your moment comes they'll hopefully do the same for you.

Cultural Importance

In the past black people didn't have the freedom to assemble. Even after we were "freed" and tried to assemble, there were laws and injunctions that prevented it. Now that we can assemble, we should do so, especially when it's in support of our own.

> **"If you enter this world knowing you are loved and you leave this world knowing the same, then everything that happens in between can be dealt with." — Michael Jackson**

BUSINESS & FINANCE

The entrepreneur spirit is alive and well within the black community. The problem is that we are so splintered into clicks that it's hard for most of us to network with people that look like us. This is why we often end up seeking loans from people that don't look like us. They don't want to loan us money in the first place, so they either deny our loans or we get penalized with higher than normal interest rates. As a community, we need to work on our business and financial intelligence so that when we're ready to make moves, we don't have to go to people that don't look like us and ask for their help to open businesses in our own community.

> **"Life is like business, 20 percent of what happens to you is 80 percent of how you react." – Daymond John**

#18. Be Financially Conscious

The first step in reaching any financial goals we have is to be financially conscious. That means we need to know when money is coming in, how much money is coming in, how much is going back out, and how much we're keeping at the end of every month. Understanding the cycle of how we spend money will help us plug any leaks to our income.

- Create a list of your monthly expenses.
- Subtract those expenses from what you bring in every month.

- How much do you have left?

If the amount of money you should have left doesn't match the amount of money that you have available to you, go back to your expense list and figure out what you missed.

In addition to knowing where our money is going, we also need to be aware of who we're spending our money with. We should try to spend money with people that look like us and live in our own community, before spending with everyone else. There's a reason every city has a "Chinatown" but all we have is "the hood". When we spend more money outside of our neighborhoods, the following happens:

- The people we spend our money with, turn around and spend our money in their own communities, with people that look like them.
- The businesses in our neighborhoods slowly die out.
- Empty shopping centers are worthless and bring down property value.
- People that don't look like us buy up our neighborhoods for a cheaper price and begin gentrifying it.
- Gentrification eventually raises the property value higher than it was originally was, forcing rents higher.
- With higher rents, we can no longer afford to live in our own communities.

"Rich Dad Poor Dad" and "The Cashflow Quadrant" are two great books that will help get you started with financial literacy. They've influenced many people, including myself, to step up our understanding of finance.

Cultural Importance

A lot of our athletes have been taken advantage of and lost millions due to not being financially aware. The same goes for black business owners that have been diluted out of companies or outright robbed by contract. If people are taking percentages, know what that percentage is. People that don't look like us view us as weak and easy to take advantage of because we have poor money habits. Poor money habits are a choice, but they don't have to be our future choice.

> **"Anyone who has ever struggled with poverty knows how extremely expensive it is to be poor." - James Baldwin**

#19. Be Credit Conscious

According to the stereotype, black people have bad credit, but we don't have to succumb to that stereotype. Understanding how credit works is important if you plan to start a business or buy property in your own name. One of the best resources available can be found online for free.

- www.creditboards.com

Good and bad credit aren't based on skin color. They're actually based on debt to loan ration and paying our bills on time. There are other facts such as length of credit history, but that will work itself out as long as we stay on top of the other two factors. Having good credit will help you if you ever want to:

- Get loans for real estate.
- Get a loan to start a business.
- Lower your interest rates so you pay less for loans.

While you're on the road to good credit, don't fall for the short cuts. There are people that will claim to be able to fix your credit, but many of them are just preying on a lack of knowledge. Be careful of who you hand your money over to.

Cultural Importance

Our historical lack of good credit has held us back from acquiring land, businesses, and even achieving home ownership. Statistically, home ownership is tied to generational wealth accumulation, which is why there is such a wealth gap between black Americans and everyone else. If we educate ourselves on credit, we can close the wealth gap without relying on the government to do anything for us.

> **"You wanna know what's more important than throwin' away money at a strip club? Credit."**
> **– Jay Z**

#20. Embrace Entrepreneurship

We should all aspire to own our own businesses so that we don't have to answer to people that don't look like us. Not only that, we can hire people that look like us and start to solve our own unemployment rate. We don't need government assistance to do something that we're more than capable of doing ourselves.

The internet has leveled the playing field in almost all arenas, especially when it comes to business. For only $12 anyone can set up their own website or blog, and monetize it. Websites and blogs are the digital equivalent to a store front, but with less risk and more reward.

- Wordpress is the best content management system (CMS) available, and it's free.
- Affiliate programs pay out a commission if you send customers to their site, which means you don't have to purchase any inventory or store space.

- Google will pay you to run ads on your site through their Adsense program.

Owning a digital storefront allows anyone to make money while they continue to work their full time job. It's not easy money and still has to be run like a business. There's a learning curve and anyone not committed won't follow through. Regardless of the outcome, the opportunities are out there for us to "play catch up" financially, but we have to take the first step and get started. Imagine if we put in the same 40+ hours per week building our own online business as we do working at other people's businesses.

- Find like minded people and build an online business together.
- Have everyone choose a different aspect of business and then read everything you can find about the subject. Watch YouTube as well.
- Always do the right thing when it comes to your partners and your customers, because bad reviews on the internet are forever.

A lot of this ties back into Law #10. The reason the importance of online ownership is stressed is because money and credit tend to be an issue in our community. The internet requires less than $20 to get started and there are no credit checks. Affiliate programs are free to join, and give you immediate access to inventory from all over the web. It doesn't have to be a permanent option, but it's great as a vehicle for getting where we'd like to go.

Cultural Importance

In the past our people owned our own businesses and even had our own towns. Mostly because most white business owners wouldn't hire a black person or sell us goods. We had very few options but to become entrepreneurs, farmers, and entertainers.

> **"Success is the result of perfection, hard work, learning from failure, loyalty, and persistence."**
> **— Colin Powell**

#21. Create Generational Wealth

We talk about generational wealth, but the majority of us don't know how to create it. This is why we need to educate ourselves on the different types of income.

- **Pay For Time:** You get an hourly rate or salary. Once you stop working you stop getting paid.
- **Passive Income:** Money that can be made while you sleep or go out with your friends.
- **Residual Income:** This income is based on renting housing units, dividends from investments, and offering subscription services.

Two good books that are great places to start are "Rich Dad Poor Dad" and "The Cashflow Quadrant", both written by Robert Kiyosaki. Understanding the basic flow of money is the first step in creating personal and generational wealth. We also need to define what wealth means to us on a personal level.

- Do you want to have millions of dollars saved in a bank?
- Do you want to have millions of dollars in property?
- Do you want to pay off your house and leave enough residual income for your children to not have to work for anyone else?

None of these are bad options and all of them are achievable if we understand what it takes to achieve our goals.

Cultural Importance

The ability to pass down generational wealth is why our community keeps falling further and further behind. It is our responsibility to start building something that generates income and pass it on, even if it's just an online business that brings in a consistent $1,000 per month without having to work hourly for it. The goal is to leave our children something that they can build on without starting from scratch. Just think for a moment how different your life would be if you started out with a guaranteed $1,000 per month on top of your work income. We need to do our best to make that a reality for the next generation.

> **"Cause you could have all the chips, be poor or rich, still nobody want a brother having shhhh. If I ruled the world and everything in it, sky's the limit, I'd push a Q-45 Infinit. It wouldn't be no such thing as jealousies or B Felonies Strictly living longevity to the destiny."**
> **- Nasir Jones**

#22. Invest In Real Estate

There are some things we do as a culture that adds to the wealth gap in this country. Instead of putting pressure on our kids to move out at age 18, we should encourage them to stay long enough to save up a down payment for a house or condo.

- Buying is cheaper than renting in most cases.
- Home ownership encourages long term responsibility.
- Paying a mortgage on time improves credit.

It's much harder to save for down payment on a house while paying the landlord's mortgage. We often make fun of how many Mexicans live in a house or ride in a car, but they do very well financially. Many own their own businesses and houses because they have a tighter knit family unit than most black homes. Some states offer down payment assistance, reimbursement, and other incentives for first time home buyers. We need to familiarize ourselves with these programs and start taking advantage of them.

Cultural Importance

In the past we weren't allowed to own land, and even after we got the right to own land, we weren't allowed to own it in certain neighborhoods. Owning our own real estate means that we don't have to put thousands of dollars per year into the pockets of people that don't look like us.

> **"I just thought everybody lived around abandoned buildings and crack-heads, ... I lived in the ghetto until I was like 19. I came to (Los Angeles), stayed at hotels and stuff. When I got back and I saw what my neighborhood looked like, I started getting scared." – Chris Rock**

#23. Invest In Our Children

We often think of investing in our children as saving up for their college education, but kids aim a lot higher these days. Here are some examples of investing in our children in the modern age:

- If your kid like to entertain, dance, sing, etc., set their room up to film videos for YouTube so they can get paid for it.
- If your kid wants to write a children's book, get on Fiverr, learn how to self publish, and make it happen.

If we invest in our kid's dreams early on, they'll have plenty of time to grow their business or brand. If they turn out to be successful, they'll be able to pay their way through college without having to start out their adult life tens of thousands of dollars in debt because of student loans.

Cultural Importance

In the past we had very limited choices in what we could be. Our jobs were limited to mostly labor or entertaining Europeans. Thankfully things have gotten a lot better and future generations will have a lot more options.

> **"I knew that I lived in a country in which the aspirations of black people were limited, marked-off. Yet I felt that I had to go somewhere and do something to redeem my being alive." — Richard Wright**

#24. Don't Be A Hater

As a people we have a bad habit of saying something negative about someone when someone else gives them a compliment. Many times we aren't even conscious of it. We could come up with a ton of scenarios to prove the point, but the point is, we need to stop knocking each other just because someone else has something good to say about someone else. This is the very definition of being a hater. There's a difference between not liking someone and being a hater, and the need to follow a compliment with an insult is being a hater.

Cultural Importance

This is the same mentality that the media has about black victims. They do it when one of us gets killed, by digging up every bit of dirt they can.

We do it while people are alive, if they reach a certain level of success. We can't control what the media does, but we can control how we choose to conduct ourselves.

> **"I have learned that success is to be measured not so much by the position that one has reached in life as by the obstacles which he has had to overcome while trying to succeed."**
> **– Booker T. Washington**

#25. Read Every Contract

One of the biggest ways we get taken advantage of in business is by not reading contracts. We've all heard the stories from entertainers, but it can happen in other industries as well. Always make sure you read your contracts for yourself and ask the following questions:

- What do they expect from you?
- What should you expect from them?
- What is the duration of the contract?
- How do you get out of the contract if necessary?

After you read the contract for yourself, take it to an attorney not associated with the person or business you're thinking about signing a contract with. One of the best ways to understand something is to try it yourself. Get online and learn how to write the kind of contracts you'll be dealing with. The process will help you become familiar with the terminology, and you'll be able to identify if something doesn't look right in the fine print.

While we're dealing with contracts, we should talk about treating people fairly in business. There's more than enough money to go around, and running a shady business that preys on ignorance isn't necessary.

We should always try to be fair in our business practices, especially when dealing with our own people. If we empower them, they may be in the position to help us if we ever need it, but when we take advantage of people we burn those bridges forever.

Cultural Importance

Contracts have been used by Europeans to steal millions (possibly billions) in wealth from our people. They count on us not knowing or understanding the terms, which is how they get over on our athletes and entertainers that don't have good representation.

> **"I believe everyone in the world is born with genius-level talent. Apply yourself to whatever you're genius at, and you can do anything in the world." – Jay Z**

#26. Learn How To Invest

At a basic level the concept of investing is straightforward. We put money at risk in hopes of making a small profit. The following are just a few ways that we can invest our money:

1. Stocks
2. Bonds
3. REITS
4. Funds
5. Crowd Lending

Becoming a successful investor allows us to put our money to work for us, which increases our overall earning potential. Before choosing any kind of investment, we need to educate ourselves about what we plan to invest in.

- Minimum investment.
- Time it takes to sell the asset.
- Expected return on investment (ROI).
- How much risk is involved.
- Tax implications.

In addition to the above, we need to educate ourselves on how much commission or per trade fee is charged whenever we buy, sell, or trade an asset.

Cultural Importance

Other cultures teach their kids about investing at an early age, while we embrace a culture of wasteful spending. Much of our wealth has been given away to white clothing designers, white owned liquor companies, white owned jewelry companies, and white owned clubs. If we're going to spend our money on their stuff, we should spending owning a piece of the company instead of just being consumers of their products.

> **"One thing that's true is that whether you are making a financial investment or an investment of the heart, you usually get what you give. What's also true is that investing the wrong assets into the wrong places is a great way to end up broke (or broken)." – Dr. Boyce Watkins**

#27. Invest In Yourself First

The best investment you can ever make is to invest in yourself. If you want to start a business, go to school, read books, watch YouTube, or whatever it is you need to do to make it happen. The cold hard fact is that we can't expect other people to invest in us if we aren't willing to first invest in ourselves.

- Invest the time to write out a five year plan.
- Invest the time to write a plan to achieve the goals in your five year plan.
- Invest the money to achieve the goals in your five year plan.

Investing in ourselves a little bit at a time eventually adds up. We don't need large sums of money to make life changing investments. We just need time, patience, a plan, and the willingness to bet on ourselves.

- If you want to record an album, start by recording one song per month.
- If you want to start a business, start by fixing your personal credit.
- If you want to be a professional athlete, start by training every day.

Even if you don't see immediate results, they'll start to manifest as you get closer to reaching your five year goal.

Cultural Importance

This is just another piece of good advice that transcends culture. We spend a lot of time working to pay other people, which leaves little left over for saving or furthering our goals. We should invest in ourselves first and everyone else after.

> **"I used to always run off at the mouth and talk about people. I just didn't know that it would make a living for me." - D. L. Hughley**

#28. Leave More Than Bills

When we pass, more often than not, we leave debt and funeral expenses to our family as an inheritance. If we plan to leave more than hardship, we must understand why it is so important for us to handle our business while we're still alive.

- We must try our hardest to pay off our debts.
- We must try our hardest to give our children and grandchildren a head start.
- We must pass on our knowledge about finance, entrepreneurship, and personal responsibility to future generations.

All of the above are why we must start businesses or websites that generate income. By establishing sources of income that can be passed on, it ensures that our sons and daughters don't have to beg people that look like us for jobs. They don't have to tip toe around people that don't like them for fear of losing their only source of income.

- We must make sure that we have life and health insurance.
- We must make sure that we have a will and power of attorney.

If you do not yet have the above in place, make sure you consult an attorney to help get your affairs in order.

Cultural Importance

Most of us have seen people on the corner taking donations for funerals that the family can't afford to pay for. Our people fail to prepare for death more often than not, which puts our families in a bad financial position. At the very minimum we should seek to eliminate that burden.

> **"I think if we are actually going to accept our generation's responsibility, that's going to mean that we give our children no less retirement security than we inherited from our parents." – Carol Moseley Braun**

COMMUNITY

There is history in the black community because we have always been segregated from white society. Even after the end of Segregation, our people couldn't get approved from home loans in white neighborhoods or were often run out of white neighborhoods if they did manage to buy a home there. This has allowed our communities to develop a rich history that many of our people want to run away from instead of invest in. This mentality is leading to Gentrification all over the United States. People that don't look like us are buying up the property for cheap in our neighborhoods, building it up, raising rents, and forcing us out. As a community we need to come together or the fact is they'll eventually push us out until our history and the little unity we have are just distant memories.

> *"I believe in the brotherhood of all men, but I don't believe in wasting brotherhood on anyone who doesn't want to practice it with me."*
> **– Malcolm X**

#29. Be Socially Conscious

We need to know what's going on in society in general, but in our own communities specifically. It's our responsibility to know who is behind which movement and what their motivations are behind starting that movement. While black unity is important, the mob mentality shouldn't influence whether or not we support a movement.

- Which communities have the most Planned Parenthoods?
- Which communities have the most fertility clinics?
- Which communities have the most liquor stores?
- Which communities have the most gun stores?

- Which communities have the most police?

Being aware of the above allows us to understand why some things are the way they are, and why certain ideologies in word don't match the actions that we see (politics, organizations, etc.).

Cultural Importance

At one time our own communities were all we had, which meant that we were tied into what was going on. As we've been able to get higher paying jobs and make a little more money, some of our people move away and lose touch with what's still going on all over America.

> **"Our records, if you have a dark sense of humor, were funny, but our records weren't about comedy. They were about protests, fantasy, confrontation and all that." – Ice Cube**

#30. Be Politically Conscious

Politics is a touchy subject for a lot of people because we've been conditioned to believe that we need to support one of the two main parties. Knowing a party's history allows to see that there is a consistency to the policies they pass. Understanding what they stand for allows us to see whether they are for us or against us.

- MLK was opposed to abortion. Which party is opposed to MLK's beliefs?
- The Black Panthers were pro 2nd Amendment and encouraged black people to exercise it. Which party opposes what the Panthers stood for?
- Which party was opposed to ending Segregation?
- Which party supports mass incarceration?

- Which party supports the drug war?
- Which party passed the Crime Bill, which increased the racist effects of the war on drugs?

We need to stop making excuses for parties when they wrong our communities. When we get honest about our situation, then we can make political progress. Until then, we just keep voting for our own demise at the hands of people who've shown us that they don't care about our community.

Cultural Importance

In the past, our people knew what was going on in politics and kept up with whether or not politicians were delivering on their promises. Now we seem to only be interested every couple of years, know very little about candidates other than political party, and make no effort to hold our representatives to their promises. This has allowed the black community to be shoved to the back of the line behind immigration, LGBTQ rights, gun laws, and everything else that pops up.

> **"What America was built on was being able to say, 'Hey, we're going to come in and use our resources to build for ourselves and our communities and build around that. We're not going to depend on others." - Common**

#31. Give Back To Our Community

We need to start creating our own social programs that add to the community. The current trend seems to be starting a non-profit, but it's expensive and many rarely give back as much as they take in. What we need are low cost for-profit programs that enrich our communities.

An example of this would be a community basketball league. All anyone would need are a few people willing to coach, people willing to play, and people willing to referee. Practices could be held at a park for zero cost. Team uniforms can be something as simple as different solid bright colored shirts (no gang colors). This would give kids and teenagers in the community something to do and could be funded out of pocket by a handful of adults. There are other kinds of community programs we can run as well, if we just get creative.

Cultural Importance

If we gave back to our own communities, we wouldn't have to rely on the government for grants or anything else. Controlling how much funding we receive is one way for the government to ensure that our neighborhoods only progress as much as they want them to. When we take it upon ourselves to get things done, they can no longer continue to limit our growth.

> **"That's how we do it in the black community; we give back to the people who made us who we are. We never forget that." – Snoop Dogg**

#32. Shop Black Whenever Possible

This is easier said than done for many reasons. The biggest two being convenience and transportation. However, whenever possible we should always try to support our own people first. We spend a lot of time idolizing white owned brands that don't give anything back to our communities:

- Versace
- Ferrari
- Gucci

The list goes on and on, but what happened to FUBU? Why is it that our community will give eternal longevity to white owned brands, but our black owned brands are "played out?" Support up and coming black clothing lines, shoe lines, grocery stores, publishing companies, etc. If we make sure that our own people are in a better position, they may in turn be able to help more of our people get into a better position, which goes into Law #33.

Cultural Importance

There was a time when we could only shop black in some places. Now that we can shop anywhere, we choose to give our money to the same people that refuse to come shop in or live in our neighborhoods. We need to keep black dollars in black hands for as long as possible.

> **"So our people not only have to be reeducated to the importance of supporting black business, but the black man himself has to be made aware of the importance of going into business. And once you and I go into business, we own and operate at least the businesses in our community. What we will be doing is developing a situation wherein we will actually be able to create employment for the people in the community. And once you can create some employment in the community where you live it will eliminate the necessity of you and me having to act ignorantly and disgracefully, boycotting and picketing some practice someplace else trying to beg him for a job." – Malcolm X**

#33. Pull Our People Up

If your job is looking for employees, suggest friends or family members that you know will be good for the job. If you're in a management position, hire more of our people. Other races do it already, which is why you'll see mostly Caucasians at a Caucasian owned company. The Chinese have a "Chinatown" in almost every city in America, but we have "the hood" or "the ghetto."

When we support our own businesses in our own neighborhoods, they're more likely to hire our own people from our own neighborhoods. This naturally leads to lower unemployment and lower poverty within our communities. While I do not condone drug dealing, if drug dealers reinvested their money into the neighborhoods they live in, it would go a long way in making our neighborhoods better.

Cultural Importance

Our people are often compared to crabs in a barrel. If we put a bunch of crabs in a bucket, every time there's a chance of one escaping, another one pulls him back down. When we get free, we need to reach back down and pull more of our people up.

> **"There is always something to do. There are hungry people to feed, naked people to clothe, sick people to comfort and make well. And while I don't expect you to save the world I do think it's not asking too much for you to love those with whom you sleep, share the happiness of those whom you call friend, engage those among you who are visionary and remove**

from your life those who offer you depression, despair and disrespect." - Nikki Giovanni

#34. Embrace Positive Language

This isn't an appeal to stop using the "N" word, but more of an appeal to start using more positive language. Why is it necessary for us to encourage calling each other beasts, gorillas, apes, goons, and savages? These are the same derogatory terms that we get upset about when they're said about us by people that don't look like us.

It's a cop out to say that we're claiming those words and turning them around, when in reality, they're dictating the next thing we call ourselves. That's not taking control, that's being manipulated. Now, whenever we turn on the radio, we're bombarded with nothing but negative labels for our people over and over again.

- **Savage:** (chiefly in historical or literary contexts) a member of a people regarded as primitive and uncivilized.

Our people were far from savages, and I doubt anyone's mother born before the year 2000 would proudly proclaim that they raised their children to think of themselves as savages... and yet here we are as a people. We're brothers and sisters, kings and queens, and much more than that. We need to start replacing all of our negative language with positive terms that don't empower the police to murder us because they look at us as savages.

Cultural Importance

We can turn on the news any given day and see our people called "thugs", even when we're the victims. The white media calls our women "welfare queens" and "nappy headed hoes", and we still turn around and do it to each others. We need to give more thought to the words we say and how we want our people to feel about themselves based on the words the come out of our mouths.

> **"I always bear in mind that my mission is to leave behind me the kind of impression that will make it easier for those who follow."**
> **- Marian Anderson**

#35. Celebrate Black Excellence

In addition to positive language, let's celebrate each other's success. Like it, share it, and shout it out. We share everything else on social media, so we should be able to share black excellence without a moment of hesitation... and not just celebrity accomplishments. Especially when it comes to our friends, family, and people that live in our local communities.

Cultural Importance

When James Shaw stopped "The Waffle House Shooter", our president ignored his heroism, but the President made sure to call Nazi sympathizers "good people". Even when our people do something as heroic as stopping a mass shooter with their bare hands, they get ignored. We need to celebrate our own excellence regardless of whether the white media or president acknowledge us or not.

> **"You can only become accomplished at something you love. Don't make money your goal. Instead pursue the things you love doing and then do them so well that people can't take their eyes off you." – Maya Angelou**

#36. Share What You Know

Knowledge is power. Therefore by sharing knowledge, we're sharing power. If we can offer input, direction, or advice that will help our people better themselves, then we should feel OBLIGATED to help them. This is not to be confused with consulting for free or giving away services you normally charge for, but sharing tips or offering advice on occasion has a residual effect.

- You help them.
- They become better.
- They help someone else.
- And so on...

The small act of sharing what you know, even if you believe it is insignificant, can have a huge positive effect on our community.

Cultural Importance

Sharing what we know has always been how we educated each other, when we weren't allowed a formal education. We need to continue this tradition by sharing what we know when we get the chance.

> **"It's easy to love somebody. Sit with them a little bit and talk to them a while."**
> **– Richard Pryor**

#37. Support Local Talent

No matter where you live in the world, there's always someone local and talented looking for an opportunity. Support them as much as possible. Too often we let white controlled radio and TV tell our people what's "hot", who we should be listening to, and what we should be spending our money on.

- If you work for radio, give local musicians a chance to be heard.
- If you work for or own an art gallery, give local artists a chance to be featured in your gallery.
- If you own a clothing store, offer aspiring designers consignment. You get inventory and free profit and they get to distribute their products. It's a win / win.

By supporting local talent, they're likely going to spend their money locally and hopefully with our people. If those local artists blow up, hopefully they'll remember where they came from and reinvest it in their own communities.

Cultural Importance

In the past our people couldn't travel freely to hear talent from all over the country, so their only option was to support local talent. Now that we have the option to hear more, we ignore local talent completely.

> **"Whether it's freedom to express, freedom to live, freedom to earn, freedom to thrive, freedom to learn, whatever it is, I want to make sure that I'm a part of these spaces and opening doors." – Angela Rye**

#38. Give Back To Our People

If you see our people in need and it's within your power to help without jeopardizing your safety or financial well being, do so without hesitation.

- Help our homeless people.
- Hold doors for our women, children, and men.
- Donate directly to families in your community in addition to giving to charities and non profits for small things like food and clothes.
- Treat each other with basic respect.

This Law is especially important for successful celebrities and business owners. Don't just take from the community until you make it and then forget about the people that supported you. After you reach a certain level of success, start giving back even if it's in small ways.

- Perform for free at fundraisers.
- Donate art for fundraisers.
- Start an internship at your business.
- Feed the homeless on Taco Tuesdays.

The above are just a few examples of cheap and no cost actions that many celebrities can do to help the community.

Cultural Importance

The concept of paying it forward isn't new. None of us has made it to where we are in life without the help of someone. Someone gave us a job, a promotion, or invested, or gave us an opportunity of some kind. We should pay it forward to our own people when we can.

> **"How far you go in life depends on your being tender with the young, compassionate with the aged, sympathetic with the striving, and tolerant of the weak and strong. Because someday in your life you will have been all of these." – George Washington Carver**

#39. Taking Back Our Communities

Within our own communities there are people that terrorize, murder, rape, and have no other purpose than to destroy what little we have. These people need to understand that they are no longer welcomed.

- We need to start our own neighborhood watch programs.
- We need to form our own neighborhood watch patrols.
- We need to start reporting major criminal activity.

We pay taxes and we should use the police to strategically take back our communities by only reporting the most egregious offenses such as rape, murder, home invasion, etc. When it comes to fights, we should stop instigating and encouraging fighting between our own people.

Most of us have seen Django, and the two slaves forced to fight for the entertainment of white people is based on reality. All we have to do is look at boxing to see that it just evolved into a big business. If two people insist on fighting, set it up at a local gym, have the fight, and be done with it after.

Cultural Importance

Our own communities use to be the safest place for our people, and still should be. If we police our own communities, we don't have to rely on white people to police our communities for us.

> **"It's our responsibility for the village to say, 'Hey we're going to create these programs,' whether it's sports, creative arts, music, we need some things to give young people positive things to do, and that's including jobs."**
> **- Common**

#40. The Repurposing of Gang Culture

Just observe how we treat each other compared to how we treat people that aren't us. We treat us the worst. That has to stop because a house divided against itself cannot stand. As part of that, black on black gang violence has to stop. Gangs don't even have to disband. If gang leaders were willing to REPURPOSE gangs into independent organizations similar to the original Black Panthers, our neighborhoods would change overnight.

- Gangs already have leadership in place.
- Gangs already have people committed to a common cause.
- Gangs already have enough firepower to protect their neighborhoods.

If the purpose of joining the gang is for protection, then what's wrong with protecting black people in general, regardless of what neighborhood they live in? White people are murdering black people in public in broad daylight because many of them are at war with us. Instead of fighting and killing each other, we should be coming together to PROTECT each other. This is NOT a call to wage war on white people, but a wakeup call to be aware that we need to be unified for survival.

Cultural Importance

People join gangs for different reasons, and repurposing gangs is much better than calling the cops to have our own people locked up or killed. Our people have always grouped up for safety, but we never had to group up to stay safe from each other. It shouldn't be that way now and it doesn't have to remain that way.

> **"Not everything that is faced can be changed, but nothing can be changed until it is faced."**

— James Baldwin

#41. Stop Begging For Equality

Our people have been trying to beg, plead, protest, riot, and vote our way into being treated as human for 400 years, and all we have to do is look around to see how people that don't look like us feel about us. We can't force people to not hate us and we should stop begging them for equality.

- The Democrats don't deserve our votes until they meet our demands.
- The Republicans don't deserve our votes until they meet our demands.
- We should vote for whoever is willing to actually meet our demands.

The reason we don't make any progress is because we've been brainwashed to believe we must vote and that vote must be Democrat. But let's look at how other groups handle voting.

- Unions withhold their votes and support unless they have certain demands met by local candidates.
- Asians, Latinos, and European Jews all withhold their vote and support until their needs are met.
- The LGBTQ community withholds their vote from any party that isn't supporting them.

The black community is the ONLY community that refuses to withhold our vote unless we get something in return. Democrats are not entitled to our votes regardless of what they believe. It is mostly due to Democrat legislation that we have such a high incarceration rate and poverty gap compared to other groups. Some of the demands we should consider would be:

1. Repeal mandatory minimum prison sentences.
2. Repeal privatized prisons.
3. Require probation for minor non violent crimes.
4. Automatically seal records after 5 years for misdemeanors and 7 years for felonies.
5. Automatically restore voting rights for felons after 7 years.
6. Create laws to require policing to reflect the demographics of a neighborhood (ex. 80% black = 80% black police).
7. No paid leave for police after shooting someone. If they are cleared of all charges, then they must receive back pay.
8. Establish a civilian investigation board to handle potential crimes committed by police.
9. All juries must be racially balanced and no less than three of the jurors must be of the accused person's own race.
10. Amend the 13th Amendment to read that slavery is abolished and CANNOT be used as punishment for a crime.

If either of the main parties can't or simply won't meet our demands, then we don't vote for them. The other half of our problem is that our own people subvert our cause by throwing away votes for the sake of throwing away votes. Not only do they throw away the vote, they blame non voters for not voting, even though Democrats make no attempt to earn the non voter vote. If they want to earn our vote, they can meet our demands or lose more elections. We should not be helping them win elections if they aren't helping our community... period.

Cultural Importance

Politicians make lots of promises to the black community, and it's rare that they follow through. We need to stop letting them get away with it and finally take a stand. Otherwise we'll never make any progress as a people.

> **"The burden of being black is that you have to be superior just to be equal. But the glory of it is that, once you achieve, you have achieved, indeed." – Jesse Jackson**

#42. Create Our Own Opportunities

There are plenty of opportunities to start our own businesses, go to school, and more now that the internet has connected most of the world. An online storefront is a cheap and easy way to go into business without the risk involved with opening a storefront.

- If it's hard to book radio interviews or get your music played, try approaching small to mid size podcasts.
- If you can't afford to advertise on a billboard, use Google Adwords and advertise on websites.
- If you can't afford to buy inventory, use affiliate programs to earn a commission for sending customers to Amazon, Target, Walmart, etc.

Now that Google exists, saying "I don't know" is just an excuse for not knowing how to do something. We need to capitalize on this opportunity and start creating our own opportunities.

Cultural Importance

There were certain industries we weren't allowed to work our way into in the past. Now we can start businesses in almost any industry we want. The internet allows us to disrupt multiple industries without having to spend millions of dollars to do it.

> **"I believe in destiny. But I also believe that you can't just sit back and let destiny happen. A lot**

> of times, an opportunity might fall into your lap, but you have to be ready for that opportunity. You can't sit there waiting on it. A lot of times you are going to have to get out there and make it happen." - Spike Lee

#43. Mentor A Young Person

We need more mentors in our community so that our young people stop looking up to pimps, drug dealers, etc. There are already programs set up like Big Brothers Big Sisters that we can volunteer our time with if we don't have family members that we can mentor. A lot of times a mentor can help youth avoid gangs, help prepare for college, and even point them in the right direction to achieve their goals.

Mentors for kids are great, but there are adults that need career mentorship as well. It is up to us to help people in our community take the right path, especially if we're involved in a career that they aspire to be in.

Cultural Importance

Between racist laws, police killing our men, and negative aspects of entertainment culture, a lot of homes are lacking men as mentors. It's up to us to end that cycle by going out of our way to counter their assault on our community. On the career side of that, people that don't look like us usually aren't looking for people that look like us for them to mentor. We need to have our own back when it comes to mentorship.

> "As an African-American male born with a couple of strikes against you because of your skin color, I think it's very, very important to have

> **some positive role models around, especially male influences."**
> **– Omari Hardwick**

ACTIVISM

Activism has been part of the black American experience since the beginning. We rebelled on board the slave ships, we rebelled on the plantations, we rebelled during the Civil War, we rebelled during the Watts Riots, we rebelled during the L.A. Riots, and we'll continue to rebel until we achieve our ultimate goal, which is complete freedom.

There is something inside of all of us that craves total autonomy from the system of white supremacy. We weren't created to subjected to them, and therefore it is in our nature to rebel against them. While rebellion always requires an act of defiance, those acts do not always need to be visible to the general public. Out of sight, out of mind.

#44. Master Solo Activism

Something that I learned from reading Sun Tzu's "The Art of War" was to remain formless so that the opposition never knows what you're going to do. MLK was killed because he organized, publically defied white authority, and had the nerve to lead other black people in rebellion. Malcolm was murdered for the same reason. The Panthers were murdered and imprisoned for the same reason.

- A movement can be destroyed but an ideology cannot.
- Black leaders can be destroyed but an ideology cannot.

We should all be leaders of our own personal protests, rallies, etc. We as individuals should all be united in common goal of equality. When we see each other wronged, our values should be so important to us as individuals that we don't need to wait for someone else to call for a boy-cott or draw the attention of the world. We've drawn the world's attention countless times and yet nothing has changed. In fact, after the Starbuck's boycott, the CEO went on TV and bragged that they hadn't lost a dime in revenue. Out of principle everyone of us should've continued the boycott without another word having to be said. He was letting the world know that his employees can treat us however they want and they can fix it all with a fake apology. Activism doesn't begin or end with boycotting:

- If you're a hiring manager, hire more of our people to work in their businesses.
- If you have a chance to promote someone to a higher position, promote one of our people.
- If you're in a position of power and it won't jeopardize your job to ignore small offenses, give our people a warning instead of reporting them.

We don't need to adopt any symbols are walk around with a balled fist in the air. We don't have to be openly pro black around those that don't look like us either. As long as our actions are pro black, they don't need to know what's going on right in front of their faces. Remain formless.

Cultural Importance

This comes back to personal responsibility. We shouldn't give our money to people cause harm to people in our community. We've also seen how often white people call the police on us for just existing. We shouldn't be reporting each other on the job when it can be avoided.

> **"Be your own leader, be your own self, step out of my shadows and be your own person."**
> **– Snoop Dogg**

#45. Don't Let Others Dictate Our Culture

We need to stop embracing non black people that make a mockery of our culture by becoming a caricature of what they believe black culture to be.

- White girls with butt injections, implants, rapping, and twerking in their videos shouldn't be getting a dime of our hard earned money.
- Asian males pushing gang culture and drugs to black youth shouldn't be getting a dime of our hard earned money.

The reason we have to deal with the above is because the music industry is controlled by people that are not black.

- They pay stylists to turn our rappers into stereotypes of what they think we look and dress like (sagging pants, face tats, gold grills, etc.).
- Record companies pay directors to fill music videos with guns, half naked black women to objectify, and feminized men.
- Record companies encourage and often only approve of music that reinforce black stereotypes.

When we see people attempting to infiltrate our culture by portraying stereotypes, we need to boycott their music, movies, and whatever projects they're planning to release. They know what they're doing would never be supported in their own culture, so they bring it to ours in order to poison our youth and take money out of the black community. They are the true definition of culture vultures.

- They teach us to buy jewelry instead of buying the jewelry store.
- They teach us to buy out the bar instead of buying the bar.

- They teach us to make it rain in strip clubs instead of setting up trust funds for our kids.
- They teach us to spend our money on European brand names instead of building our own brands.
- They teach us that we can only play for their sports leagues instead of starting our own sports leagues.

We need to start our own Greeting card Companies, publishing companies, record labels, amateur sports leagues, grocery stores, performance venues, and more. A shift in where our dollars are spent will shift how they behave toward us.

Cultural Importance

Europeans use to watch minstrel shows as a form of entertainment. Black people would dress up in ridiculous outfits and act like buffoons in order to portray what Europeans perceived black culture to be. The music and movie industries are doing the same thing.

> **"I'll be damned if I am going to sit and watch our kids continue to grow up believing that it's cool to be ignorant, violent, high, drunk, broke, uneducated and lazy. We must critically assess the music we love and let artists know that we will no longer tolerate the mass promotion of ideas that are hell bent on destroying our kids."**
> **– Dr. Boyce Watkins**

#46. Know Who Our Allies Are

Too often when we talk about black empowerment and black unity, we overlook the fact that there are other people outside of the black community that have been helpful in our struggle. The Abolitionists are just one example of Europeans that gave their lives to help free our ancestors from plantations. Likewise, there are people that sincerely want to help us now.

Cultural Importance

Without the Abolitionists, many slaves wouldn't have been able to set up the Underground Railroad and other escape routes. The Abolitionists had allies as well. We need to continue to build bridges and make allies if we want to progress.

> **"There's always some difference between your Latino and African-American communities. But we definitely have more similarities than differences." – Aja Brown**

#47. Know Who Our Enemies Are

Just as important as knowing who our allies are, we need to know who are enemies are. There are a lot of wolves in sheep's clothing, and our people keep falling for the deception. Our problem is that we base our decisions on emotion instead of logic.

- If a political party has a history of anti black policy, don't make excuses for it and keep trying to vote that party into power.
- If a political party has time and resources to address new problems, while putting the concerns of the black community on the back burner, then we need to stop voting that party into power.

One of the hardest things in the world to do is to get black people to stop defending white Democrats as saviors, even though it can be proven historically that they're just as bad as Republicans. The right hand is so loud and boisterous with their racism that we don't see that the left hand is the one destroying our communities with their laws.

Cultural Importance

Until 1996 the Democrat party was actively passing laws to devastate the black community. Clinton's Crime Bill and Welfare reform resulted in millions of black men in jail and put over 1.5 million black families into poverty. It doesn't help that Clinton group up in the south when radical racist Southern Democrats ran the party. In the 1970s Republicans used Southern Strategy to split the party. The radical racists left and the moderate racists remained Democrats.

> **"What we all want is public safety. We don't want rhetoric that's framed through ideology."**
> **- Kamala Harris**

#48. Stop Looking To White Leadership

We don't need Europeans to co-sign, validate, or approve of what we're doing. Part of this comes from slavery and part of it comes from over 700 years of the false portrayal of Christ being a white man. That was done to get black people to look to white "saviors" for help.

- We need to stop placing them in positions of leadership over our people in our own businesses and organizations.
- We need start putting our own people in positions of leadership whenever possible.

I'm not suggesting that we don't work with Europeans or hate them at all, but that we make sure that our people see us as the decision makers, shot callers, HNICs, or whatever term you want to use.

Cultural Importance

Our people have historically not been in positions of power in this country. On jobs, the supervisor is almost always white. The same can be said for politics and law enforcement. Because our people are underrepresented, there is a shortage of images of our people in positions of power. We need to put us in those positions when we can.

> **"It's not about supplication, it's about power. It's not about asking, it's about demanding. It's not about convincing those who are currently in power, it's about changing the very face of power itself." - Kimberle Williams Crenshaw**

The Breakdown

The 48 Laws of Black Empowerment should not be looked at as a set of unchanging rules, but as a starting point to build upon. I'm aware that everything presented in this book cannot be accomplished by all people at all times, but we can all do those things that are within our ability to do right now.

The reason that I wrote this book is because people often ask me what my plan is since I do not support either of the major political parties. The reason for that being based on actual history and not feelings about what people say. I'd rather one party outright call me a nigger than to pass legislation that targets me for prison. I'd rather one party refer to Nazis as "good people" than to refer to me as a "super predator". Both are messed up, but the latter group will ultimately put our lives in danger. Therefore this plan is presented for those of us that want to actively change our community instead of begging either political party to help us. We don't need their help.

> *"I am America. I am the part you won't recognize...get used to me...my name, not yours; my religion, not yours; my goals, my own..."*
> **– Muhammad Ali**

Building On The 48 Laws

If this book has inspired you and you'd like to contribute to making this book better and more useful to our people, feel free to leave a suggestion in any comment section on my website. If your suggestion is added, I'll put your name in the book as a contributor.

- Let me know if you think more should be added to certain laws.
- Let me know if you think any laws should be worded different.
- Let me know if you think any laws could use more clarity.

All comments, suggestions, and questions are welcome, but not all will be added. You will not be paid for your contributions, but your contribution will be acknowledged in the back of all future editions of this book. Thank you for reading and may The Most High be with you as we continue our journey for black empowerment together.

www.BlackHistoryInTheBible.com

> **"If you're walking down the right path and you're willing to keep walking, eventually you'll make progress." – Barack Obama**

Patron Shout Outs

Al Davidson
Allison Gladney
Andre L. Mickens Sr.
Angela Adams
Anita Williams
Ann Jones
Antwan Hopkins
ARLIE LINDSEY
Ashley Dalencourt
Barbara A Norwood
Benjamin Douglas
Brandon Robinson
Branodn
Brian
Brigetta Perry
Brittany Glover
Calvin L Andrus
Calvin R. Miller
Carolyn Wesley
Carolyn Harper
Cecil Bradley
Chaapashayah Rawach
Chanda Hill
Charles Thomas
Christerpher Manuel
Christopher Houston
Christopher Vernell Norman
Clarence Willey
Clifford Jones
Clylisha Hunter
CM Ashby
Crystal Boykin
D. Kay

Danny Green
Darnell Blackshear
Darryl Thomas Sr.
Daryl Barnes
Deborah Matchett
Deborah Washington
Debra C. Cotton
Debra Walton
Denise Andreas
Derin Bepo
Diane Brice
Don
Donna-Marie Brown
Drew Kerr
Duane Flowers
Dustin Martin
Ed Hamiton
Eddie
Edmund Walton
Edwina Annette
Ernest Parham
Ernest Parham
Esther Thomas
Fondrae Tarmel Harris
Frank Lomax IV
frank williams
Freddie Montgomery
Frederick Williams
George Ng'ang'a
Gregory Daniel
Holly Blossom
Horace Ward
Hungry & Wildhearted

Iflknew Then
Ituri Kinney
Ivory Suggs
J C Rozier
Jamal J Ross
James C Ashby
James Reed
jarvis smith
Jason Stewart
Jayne Howard
Jeannette Kearney
Jenavisa Hardy
Jermaine Bell
Jesna Eaton
jessie forman
Joe Burke
John Grier
John Walker
Jojo Bonney
Joshua
Joshua Houston
Joshua stargell
Judy R Horton
Kay Henry
Keith A.Williams
Keith Wilson
Kelvin Williams
Kenya Friday
Kimber Luckey
Ko jesse
L Edward
Lala Mitc
Laura Rucker

Lavina Chaves
Lawrence Drake II
LeRoy Dunham
Linda Burnett
Loriel Mitchell
Marcus Daniels
Mariyah Israel
Mark E Landstrom
Mark Parker
Mayme Roberson
Meekhael Brooks
MICHAEL ERIC WILEY
Michael Paden
Michael Watson
michael watson
Michelle Smith
Mike Korutz
Momo50
Mr. Allan
Nikki Davis
Patrick Murphy
Paula Thomas
Penny
Peyton Gray
Phillip and Sharon Goodwin
Quintonia McKay
Reginia Tillman
Rev Robert E.Keyes
Richard D. McCreary II
Robert Watkins
Roderick Norman
Ronald E. Newton
S. Yahceph Lawrence

The Black Hebrew Awakening

Samantha Murrell
Sami McCauley
Sandy Howe
Shaquinta Beard
Sharon Dixon
Sheila Y Garland
Shirley Ann Williams
Shirley Williams
Smrrain
Sonia Grant
Sonya Chisholm
Stephanie Baskin
Stephanie Mccant
Stephanie Whittaker
Steven Johnson
Street Kollege
Tani Sanchez
Tausha Carter-Jacobs
Tenaya Dew
TEOTW Ministries
Terrence Lee
Tommy Rhodes
Trenace Lewis
Tumelo
Tyler parran
Tyron Sutton
Tyrone Crowder
Valeria Harris
Vanessa Rushin
Virginia Jimenez
Vivian Hopkins
Wallace Thomas
Wayne Williams
Xavier Brandon

Yvette Rivera
Yvonne Gaddis

The Black Hebrew Awakening

"And he said unto Abram, Know of a surety that thy seed shall be a stranger in a land that is not theirs, and shall serve them; and they shall afflict them four hundred years; And also that nation, whom they shall serve, will I judge: and afterward shall they come out with great sub-stance." – Genesis 15:13-14

For most of our lives we've been taught that the church has replaced Israel, Israel migrated and mixed with all nations, and that God no longer cares about Israel... but if that's the case, how can the church trust anything that comes out of the mouth of God if he'd just back out on all the promises made to Israel?

- God never abandoned Israel.
- Christianity did not replace the nation of Israel.
- Much of Christian doctrine was designed to reinforce white supremacy.

One of the biggest travesties of the Transatlantic Slave Trade is that black culture prior to coming to America was completely erased on purpose. What couldn't be erased was white washed until we were so uncertain of our identity.

- In the late 1400s Portugal began deporting black Hebrews to the West Coast of Africa.
- French, English, Portuguese, and German maps show The Kingdom of Judah located in Africa.
- A 1766 Spanish map has Negroland marked as "populated by Jews".

Available On Amazon

Bible Study Bookz

Notebooks With Covers That Represent Our Culture

Bible Study Bookz are lined notebooks that are perfect for the Bible study enthusiast that loves to take notes and keep them. Each notebook includes the following tables to enhance your study time.

- Biblical Lengths
- Biblical Weights
- Biblical Liquid Measures
- Biblical Dry Measures
- Biblical Money
- Biblical Time

Each book is compact, which makes it perfect for travel, and Bible Study Bookz can be stored on any bookshelf for easy keeping.

Available On Amazon

The Awakening Initiative

Thank you for reading The Black Hebrew Awakening. In an effort to awaken more of our people, I'm stealing a play from The Negro Project. Every month I'm going to send an Awakening Box to the pastors of ten black churches. The goal is to awaken the pastor so that the pastor can awaken the congregation. If you would like to help me reach more than ten pastors per month, please visit my Patreon page to read more about The Awakening Initiative.

The Awakening Box

patreon.com/dantefortson

Please Leave A Five Star Review

If you enjoyed reading this book, please leave a five star review on Amazon. Your review is important because it helps our people decide if they want to buy the book. If you believe what is written in this book is important, please take a few moments to leave a review. Thanks in advance.

Made in the USA
Coppell, TX
03 February 2021

49568251R00039